THE RUNAWAY

Robert Frost

Illustrations by Glenna Lang

David R. Godine · Publisher · Boston

For my first best friend, Ellie Frost,

and for our daughters,

Arielle Frost Hinckley & Esmé Lang von Hoffman

First published in 1998 by
DAVID R. GODINE, Publisher, Inc.
Box 450
Jaffrey, New Hampshire 03452

Library of Congress Cataloging in Publication Data
Frost, Robert, 1874-1963.
The runaway / Robert Frost ; illustrations by Glenna Lang.
p.   cm.
Summary: A poem about a colt frightened by falling snow.
1. Horses—Juvenile poetry. 2. Children's poetry, American.
[1. Horses—Poetry. 2. American poetry.] I. Lang, Glenna, ill. II. Title
PS3511.R94R86   1996
811'.52—DC20   96–13267 CIP

ISBN 1-56792-243-0

First Softcover Printing, 2003
Printed in Hong Kong by South China Printing Co.

THE RUNAWAY

Once when the snow of the year was beginning to fall,

We stopped by a mountain pasture to say, "Whose colt?"

A little Morgan had one forefoot on the wall,

The other curled at his breast. He dipped his head

And snorted at us. And then he had to bolt.

We heard the miniature thunder where he fled,

And we saw him, or thought we saw him, dim and gray,
Like a shadow against the curtain of falling flakes.

"I think the little fellow's afraid of the snow.
He isn't winter-broken. It isn't play

With the little fellow at all. He's running away.

I doubt if even his mother could tell him, 'Sakes,
It's only weather.' He'd think she didn't know!

Where is his mother? He can't be out alone."

And now he comes again with clatter of stone,
And mounts the wall again with whited eyes

And all his tail that isn't hair up straight.
He shudders his coat as if to throw off flies.

"Whoever it is that leaves him out so late,

When other creatures have gone to stall and bin,